THE ARCHANGEL

Also by John Urban

Three Songs for Children (2016)

Dusty Days (2018)

The London Notebook (2019)

THE ARCHANGEL

POEMS

by

JOHN URBAN

The Archangel
Copyright © 2021 by John Urban

All rights reserved. No part of this book may be reproduced in any form or by any electronic or mechanical means including information storage and retrieval systems, without permission in writing from the author.

Book design by River Sanctuary Graphic Arts

ISBN 978-1-952194-12-2

Printed in the United States of America

An Argument for Higher Knowledge and *The Archangel*
appeared in *being human: a quarterly*, 2021
The Alchemist appeared in *NEBO* Spring 2018
From the Woman at the Well was published in *The Broken Plate* 2021

Contact author at:
johnurb@sbcglobal.net

Additional copies available from:
www.riversanctuarypublishing.com
amazon.com

RIVER SANCTUARY PUBLISHING
P.O. Box 1561
Felton, California 95018
www.riversanctuarypublishing.com
Dedicated to the awakening of the New Earth

The mind is not a vessel to be filled,

but a fire to be ignited.

Plutarch

CONTENTS

PART ONE

Poetics 3

From the Woman at the Well 5

Gnomen 7

    I - II 7

    III - IV 9

    V - VI 11

An Argument For Higher Knowledge. 13

The Archangel 15

The Alchemist... 17

Perspectives on Truth 19

Now You See Me, Now You Don't 21

PART TWO

The Plenum 25

The Void 27

The Not-Infinite 29

As We Think 31

The Self in the World 33

The One Idea. 35

What Is, What Is Not 37

PART THREE

In Creation 41

Isis 43

The Truth of Beauty 45

On Thought 47

Perceptions, Conceptions 49

With Authority 51

Hart Crane 53

On True Thought 55

The Word 57

On Poetics 59

For William Blake 61

At The Center 63

PART ONE

Poetics

For the Orphics, Poetry was a sacerdotal Art.

*

In True Poems, Eternity trickles into Time.

*

With its net of words, a Poem is a spirit-catcher.

*

The True Poem, a pure Possession.

From the Woman at the Well

The spirit rises, the body falls.

*

Every mountain of earth contains a few diamonds.

*

If one cannot listen, one cannot learn.

*

The highest fall the furthest.

*

There are no secrets, for those who ask.

Gnomen

I

What we see is but one-half a world.

II

Matter, the Flood.

III

All things crumble, but the Idea remains.

IV

Intuition is the Eye of the Heart.

V

Even in the abyss of Matter, God is present.

VI

Truth, the tipping point.

An Argument For Higher Knowledge

World Knowledge cannot solve
The World Problem.

Corollary: The World fiddles
While the World burns.

The Archangel

Revealing reality
By severing the knot
Of appearances,
His sword of thought,
Bearing The Word,
Conquers The World.

The Alchemist

Deity is Its own solution
And is the only solution
To the enigma of the World.

Thus, for the Alchemist,
All things dissolve,
Or are resolved, in God.

Perspectives On Truth

Truth, simple, but all-encompassing.

*

Truth is One, but its expression Many.

*

Without Truth, knowledge
Would not, could not, be knowledge.

*

Truth, Dynamic, though Timeless and Unchanging.

*

Love of Truth leads to the Above.

Now You See Me, Now You Don't

Human beings observe; machines register.

Relativity and Quantum Mechanics
Are digressions from True Science.

Their concerns are not with Reality,
But with issues of Empiric Measurement.

Yet, the prevailing opinion is that these
Theories are True Depictions of Reality.

But, Truth has a human face, and arises
Not from numerics based on "observations"
Made by machines, but by means of human
Conceptions allied to human Perceptions.

PART TWO

The Plenum

Perfection, if it exists, must be
The perfection of something.

The sole exception is the Infinite
Who is Perfection Itself.

In other words, God is That
Which makes Perfection Perfect.

The Void

Since the Plenum, the Infinite God, is void
Of all finite characteristics, It may be termed,
At certain times, or, in certain contexts, The Void.

The Not-Infinite

I
Since a creation is simply the expression
Of a creator, and not the creator itself,
It is, in the measure of its being,
Less than its creator; thus, in order
That the Universe be less than
Its Infinite Creator, it must be finite.

II
On the other hand, since the Creation
Is the manifestation of an Infinite Creator,
It must, in some manner, bear the traces
Of the Infinity of That which is its Source.

This is, thus, the basis of the distinction
Between the Absolute Infinity predicated
Of Deity and the lesser infinities predicated
Of the heights and depths of Its Creation.

As We Think

Even as we think, what is thought
Is distinguished from all that is not thought.

Thus, what is not thought, by providing that
From which what is thought is distinguished,
Gives to what is thought the reality of being thought.

The Self in the World

Since the self is in the world, that which occurs
In the mind of the self also occurs in the world.

Thus, the thinking of the self, which occurs
In the mind of the self, occurs in the world.

So, according to the reality, or to the unreality,
Of what is thought, thinking contributes to,
Or takes away from, the reality of the World.

The One Idea

Since Truth is one, any True Idea
Cannot contradict any other True Idea.

All True Ideas are, thus, resolvable, one into
The other through a series of implications.

Which implications, in their final resolutions
And summations, merge into but a Single Idea.

What Is, What Is Not

That those features which a thing does not possess
Contribute as much to the determination of its nature
As those which it does possess, implies that non-being
Is as much an agent in the determination of the nature
Of a thing as is being, but, as the Source of all things,
Of those which are and of those which are not, The Infinite
Reposes ineffably beyond all Being, beyond all Non-being.

PART THREE

In Creation

In an act of creation, an Idea is, as it were,
Reflected in the Mirror of Matter.

Isis

What the womb of Space creates,
    The Fires of Time destroy.

The Truth of Beauty

I

The Human Heart, as part of a Rational Being,
Thereby possesses cognitive power;
Which power, however, is not Discursive, but Intuitive.

II

The Truth of an Intuitive utterance, statement, or assertion,
Resides in its harmony, in its unity; that is, in its Beauty.

On Thought

I

Thought, in order to be Thought, presupposes
Something to think about (perceptions), and, something
To think with (the conceptualizing intellect).

II

True Thought is angelic, androgynous, and is,
Whether Reasoned or Intuited, an agent of Reality.

III

As our Thought, through angelic action, is more and more
Empowered, so the more and more do we,
In our understanding, ascend the Pyramid of Being.

Perceptions, Conceptions

I

A percept is the exterior expression
Of an object's interior idea, and, as such,
Will suggest to attentive perception
The object's essence or interior idea;
The object's interior and exterior aspects
Thus comprehended, its reality is revealed.

II

Terrestrial perceptions are sensory intuitions,
But in the World of Ideas, that is, in the Spiritual world,
Perceptions are the same as Conceptions; in other words,
Ideas, or True Conceptions, are Supersensible Perceptions.

With Authority

I

Authority, the pressure or impress of Reality,
Usually through a person's words, written or spoken,
Upon the consciousness of another person.

II

Thus, those who possess knowledge of The Word, that is,
Those who possess Knowledge of Reality,
When they speak or write, speak or write with Authority.

Hart Crane

The shores of Perception and Conception
Are spanned by the Bridge of Truth.

On True Thought

True Thought truly bestows true freedom, and in the Life
And Light of Its Ideas we become more truly human.

True Thought is living, integral Thought—a vital force
Not only for the Mind, but for the Heart and Will as well.

This vitality proceeds from the Truth of True Thought;
In other words, from He Who is not only Truth Itself,
But Who is, also, The Great Physician, and, consequently,
Who is, for us, for Terrestrial Man, both Light and Life.

The Word

I

Since the Word of God is written in the World,
Truth is attained to when the Word
Of the Self merges with the Word of the World.

II

The Word, which is Truth Itself, is made manifest
Through the Truth of True Words.

Thus, in Truth, the Word walks among us.

On Poetics

True Poems are not written, but created;
They are the productions of Art, not Craft.

*

A Poem's disclosure of that which is Real
Is what gives the Poem its "Poetic Spark".

*

As Blake might have said, "True Poems
Are recorded in the Annals of Eternity".

*

True Poems are truly fiery things; they exist
In order to burn away the dross of the world.

For William Blake

I
All knowledge based upon Time,
Because of Time's perpetuity,
Is, by nature, incomplete, partial,
And, ultimately, false; only in Eternity
Is True Knowledge attained to.

II
Giants are born when Angels
Mate with the Minds of Men.

These Initiated are, then,
The Giants of Men.

III
Eternal Life, Eternal Delight.

At The Center

Love is the Fire
At the Center of Things

www.ingramcontent.com/pod-product-compliance
Lightning Source LLC
Chambersburg PA
CBHW032211040426
42449CB00005B/538